THE CLARENDON BIOGRAPHIES

General Editors: C. L. MOWAT and M. R. PRICE

HENRY VII

by

Derek Pitt M.A.

Senior History Master
St. John's School, Leatherhead

OXFORD UNIVERSITY PRESS

1966

Oxford University Press, Ely House, London W.1

GLASGOW NEW YORK TORONTO MELBOURNE WELLINGTON
CAPE TOWN SALISBURY IBADAN NAIROBI LUSAKA ADDIS ABABA
BOMBAY CALCUTTA MADRAS KARACHI LAHORE DACCA
KUALA LUMPUR HONG KONG

PRINTED AND BOUND IN ENGLAND BY
HAZELL WATSON AND VINEY LTD
AYLESBURY, BUCKS

CONTENTS

LIST OF ILLUSTRATIONS

The cover portrait of Henry VII was painted by an unknown artist in 1505, four years before the king's death. (*National Portrait Gallery*)

1

THE WINNING OF THE CROWN

In the preface to the Authorized Version of the Bible, published in 1611, the learned and godly authors pay an effusive tribute to James I, who had commissioned them to make the new translation. His 'sun', they say, had dispelled the clouds which overhung the land as a result of the death of Elizabeth I.

This is simply flattery of the first Stuart king; had it been applied to the first *Tudor* king it could be taken more at its face value, for in 1485 when Henry, Earl of Richmond, overthrew Richard III on Bosworth Field and thus made himself king as Henry VII there had certainly been clouds over England for many years. It was to be the new king's particular achievement to dispel those clouds and to prepare the way for the development of England under his successors.

Henry was born in 1457, three months after the death of his father, Edmund, Earl of Richmond. Edmund's parents had been a strangely assorted pair: his mother Katherine was the daughter of a king of France and the widow of Henry V of England. His father was Owen Tudor, a Welshman who had occupied a place in Katherine's household after her husband's premature death in 1422. Owen and Katherine had five children, of whom Edmund was the eldest. Edmund's wife Margaret was descended from John of Gaunt and Catherine Swynford, whose children were not legitimized until some time after their birth and even then were debarred from any claim to the English throne to which their father's

5

royal blood might have entitled them. So there was a question mark over the ancestry of Henry VII and no one could pretend that his claim to the throne on grounds of birth was a very strong one.

The fatherless boy Henry had a strange upbringing in Wales. The Wars of the Roses began while he was still very young and in 1468 he was captured in Harlech Castle by his Yorkist enemies under Lord Herbert. His uncle Jasper, who had brought him up, rescued him in 1470 and fled with him to Brittany. As the wars continued, the young Henry became the chief hope of the failing Lancastrian cause. This fact did not escape the notice of Richard III who became king in 1483 after murdering his nephew Edward V in the Tower of London. In Brittany plots were laid against Henry and in 1484, still with the devoted Jasper, he fled into France, of which Brittany was not at that time a part. Here he was joined by Lancastrians fleeing from Richard III, and in 1485 the exiles felt that the time had come to invade England in an attempt to depose Richard. Help was obtained from Charles VIII of France, but it was still only a small party that sailed from Harfleur and landed a few days later at Milford Haven in Henry's native Wales.

Shakespeare in his play *Richard III* makes Richard describe his enemies thus:

> 'A sort of vagabonds, rascals and run-aways,
> A scum of Bretons and base lackey peasants,
> Whom their o'er cloyed country vomits forth
> To desperate adventures and assur'd destruction.'

Desperate the adventure certainly was, for even with help from England and Wales Henry's army was only half the strength of the king's when they met at Market Bosworth in Leicestershire. But Richard was beset by treachery: Lord

Stanley with all his personal following went over to Henry's side soon after the battle began and others in the royal army showed little appetite for the struggle. So Richard, fighting with great and furious courage, was defeated and killed; his crown rolled under a hawthorn bush whence it was retrieved and placed on Henry's head amid shouts of 'long live King Henry the Seventh'. The Tudor dynasty had embarked upon its one hundred and eighteen years of rule.

At this time Henry was twenty-eight. Surviving portraits of him show a man of above average height, clean-shaven, with a straight firm mouth and a somewhat prominent nose. Francis Bacon in a long biographical essay published in 1621 wrote: 'His countenance was reverend and a little like a churchman; and as it was not strange or dark, nor was it winning or pleasing, but as the face of one well disposed.' The picture is not a very attractive one, yet this was the man whom Bacon called in the same essay 'a wonder for wise men'. 'What he minded, he compassed' is another significant comment of Bacon's; perhaps we may see in that hard un-relenting mouth a sign of the determination with which Henry pursued his policy of settling his family firmly upon the throne of England.

What was the state of the country in 1485? Since 1461 the crown had changed hands no less than six times. Two kings, the saintly ineffective Henry VI and the thirteen-year-old Edward V, had been murdered. Edward, with his younger brother, Richard, Duke of York, had been the victim of his ambitious uncle, Richard of Gloucester. This man had en-joyed his usurped throne for only two years before his death at Bosworth. It would therefore have been a bold man who would have wagered a large sum on Henry VII's chances of a long reign and a peaceful death at the end of it. What Henry had won by the sword he could easily lose by the sword and since Edward IV had five daughters and two nephews, all of whom were still alive in 1485, there was no lack of Yorkist candidates for the throne with better claims by birth than Henry possessed.

Too many kings had been deposed, exiled or murdered in the previous twenty-five years for the office of monarch to be highly regarded in the land. The ruler, in fact, had too often been shown to be merely 'primus inter pares', first among equals, chief baron of the realm—and not always chief as the remarkable career of Warwick the Kingmaker had shown. The weakening of the king's power and position had been one of the most important results of the Wars of the Roses, and it would be the main task of Henry VII to restore them.

The effect of the Wars upon the country and its people can easily be exaggerated. The fighting in them had been done largely by the powerful nobles with their armed servants or retainers. The peasant in the fields and the townsman in his shop had felt little of the Wars' impact unless one or other of the contending armies chanced to light upon the village or town in which he lived. Then he might be robbed of all he possessed, his crops seized, or his shop ruthlessly plundered. If he was lucky, however, the Wars would pass him by; it mattered little to him whether a Yorkist or a Lancastrian occupied the throne. Indeed trade had actually flourished quietly during the Wars and had been further encouraged during the period when Edward IV reigned unchallenged from 1471 to 1483. Edward himself had then participated in the wool trade with Flanders and had numbered London merchants among his friends.

Trade might continue almost unhindered in time of civil war, but law and order could not be enforced if the king whose task it was to enforce them was engaged in conflict. In these circumstances there was little chance of checking the

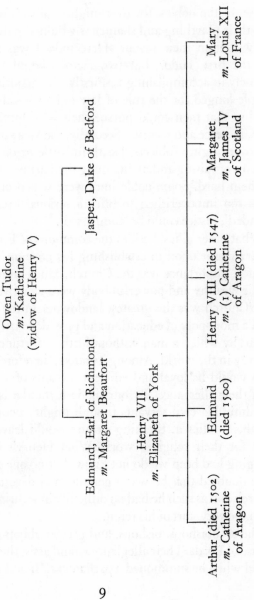

THE HOUSE OF TUDOR

Owen Tudor
m. Katherine
(widow of Henry V)

Edmund, Earl of Richmond   Jasper, Duke of Bedford
m. Margaret Beaufort

Henry VII
m. Elizabeth of York

Arthur (died 1502)   Edmund   Henry VIII (died 1547)   Margaret   Mary
m. Catherine   (died 1500)   m. (1) Catherine   m. James IV   m. Louis XII
of Aragon   of Aragon   of Scotland   of France

abuses of the nobles, the over-mighty subjects who made the law their plaything and shamelessly bullied judges and juries to twist it in their favour. Here indeed was a major task for the first Tudor, but two factors would help him immensely in accomplishing it. Firstly, the majority of English people longed for the rule of law to be re-established in the land so that men could pursue their jobs, humble or otherwise, in peace and security. Secondly, the Wars had weakened the over-mighty subjects. Death in battle or on the scaffold, the cost of raising and maintaining their armies, had hit many of them hard. Some noble lines were wiped out and others were too impoverished to offer a serious threat. If Henry 'minded', justice could be 'compassed'.

What other allies, besides the commons of England, could Henry count upon in establishing his position? Of the very greatest importance was the Church. Much would be gained if this wealthy and powerful body were won over to his side. The Church was the greatest landowner in the kingdom; it held a monopoly in education and provided virtually the only means by which a man without birth or fortune could make his way in the world. Among its ranks, therefore, were clerics who would be loyal and efficient servants of any king who won their allegiance. By our modern standards they would be admirable civil servants though mighty poor clergymen, for their duties at the king's court would leave them little time for their religious work. What Henry's religious upbringing had been we do not know, but no one ever seems to have doubted that he was a genuine and devoted son of the Church and as such he had no difficulty in securing its support from the very start of his reign.

The archbishops, bishops, and greater abbots all sat in the House of Lords. Their allegiance would assist the king greatly if and when he summoned a parliament. 'If and when', for at this period of history, parliaments were few and far between. There had to be one at the start of a reign to acknowledge the new monarch, there would have to be one if the king needed money to be raised by taxation, but a wise king would so manage his financial affairs that he could 'live of his own' without making unpopular demands upon the pockets of his subjects. As the subtle Florentine Machiavelli wrote in *The Prince* published in 1532, 'men will sooner forgive the execution of their fathers than the emptying of their own pockets'. Henry therefore used parliament as sparingly as possible and solely when it suited him.

If parliament did not govern England, who did? The answer is, the king himself with the assistance of his Council —and the members of his Council were men of his own choice together with some of the great men of the kingdom who were members by right. Edward IV had used middle-class men as a counterpoise to the over-mighty subjects on the Council and Henry followed his example in this as in many other matters. It is essential to realize that Henry was not an innovator; he made no sweeping changes nor startling breaks with the past. In his skilful unspectacular way he took the machinery of government and administration, which had served his predecessors but which had grown a little rusty during the previous decades, oiled it and set it in motion. He did not scrap it in favour of new machinery. Above all he geared it to the financial needs of the crown, for he was well aware that poverty had been a major cause of the weakness of the 15th century monarchy. So he acquired with the passage of the years, by means to be described in a later chapter, a vast fortune.

He was not a miser as his enemies during his lifetime and after suggested. A valuable insight is obtained into his life and character by a study of his Household accounts. These provide ample evidence to dispel, once and for all, the idea that he was an austere over-serious man, a stranger to pleasure, unmoved by music or other arts, sparing in his dress and diet. He would pay lavishly for delicacies for his table: 13s 4d for a large sturgeon, 5s for a pot of thyme; he would pay for his entertainments: 6s 8d to 'a fellow who swallowed coals', a few pence to 'children who sang in the royal garden', 10s to play-actors, 6s 8d to a Welsh harpist—perhaps his performance stirred childhood memories. He kept his own zoo and gave £2 13s 4d to 'one that brought the king a lion'; he was fond of a gamble and would wager on his own skill at tennis or on cards or dice. In 1502, he gave his son Henry £3 to play at dice. He was willing to pay for clothes befitting a king: 4s for a silk hatband, £30 for a collar of gold.

A large order from an Italian merchant for cloth for the king cost no less than £550 4s 2d! Even the royal hounds had to have silken collars at 3s 4d each. Ambassadors found no signs of stinginess at his Court nor was there any lack of costly ceremony on suitable occasions.

Henry was not a cruel man and in this respect compares very favourably with his son, Henry VIII. He showed mercy to poor men who found themselves, often willy-nilly, drawn into risings against him; there was no savage policy of executions such as followed the Pilgrimage of Grace in 1537 or the Rising of the Northern Earls in 1569. Even the leaders of rebellions could save their lives by paying huge fines into the King's Exchequer. It is a revealing sign of the times in which Henry lived that there were complaints about his preference for fines rather than executions, thus giving substance to Machiavelli's remark quoted earlier in this chapter. Certainly Henry was a man of remarkable moderation to be found in so brutal an age.

The population of the England he ruled cannot be accurately assessed. London was by far the largest city and may have had as many as 75,000 inhabitants. It was smaller than Paris but many foreigners thought it to be the finer city of the two. An Italian visitor noted in 1500 'in one single street leading to St Paul's, called the Strand, there are fifty-two goldsmiths' shops so rich and full of gold and silver vessels, great and small, that in all the shops of Milan, Rome, Venice and Florence put together I do not think there would be found so many of that magnificence'! This is a high compliment since Italy then was at the very peak of the wealth and artistic splendour of the Renaissance period.

Within the circle of the city wall there were ninety-seven parish churches, the spires of which were dominated by that of St Paul's itself, five hundred feet high. Near to St Paul's was the vast pile of the Tower of London, royal palace and royal prison, dominating the city as William the Conqueror had intended it should do. Many unfortunate men had endured imprisonment there or had met their fate on the scaffold erected within its walls, and many more were doomed to do so in the Tudor century. The heads of the royal victims found their last resting place upon the fortified tower at the north end of London Bridge, built in the reign of King John, and in Tudor times providing the only link between the north bank of the Thames and the flourishing 'suburb' of Southwark on the south bank. Southwark boasted a bishop's palace, yet more churches, a hospital, and before the 16th century was over it boasted also of theatres, including Shakespeare's Globe. In Southwark, as in the City, the streets were narrow, crowded, dirty and noisy, ready breeding places for the plague which was almost an annual visitor. The houses in these streets were in some cases the homes of merchants whose shops occupied the ground floor while the families, together with the apprentices, lived on the upper floors. These often overhung the streets so that it was possible to lean out of a window and shake hands with a man doing the same from his upper floor in the house opposite. Each shop had its distinctive sign to inform the passer-by of the wares for sale within and these signs were on occasions the product of highly skilled workmanship—a strange contrast to the piles of stinking rubbish in the gutters beneath them. The filth and odours of London or any other town would be quite nauseating to us to-day. Sanitation was very primitive, baths virtually unknown, and washing arrangements crude in the extreme.

Among the crowded houses of the city of London, a number of magnificent buildings stood out : these were the Halls of the various companies—the Grocers, the Goldsmiths and so on—and some of these survived the Great Fire of 1666 and even the raids of Hitler's air force to ornament modern London. Three vast halls served as markets, for the citizen of Tudor London was essentially a man of business. Even the aisles of St Paul's Cathedral were used for the conduct of affairs : a servant could be hired there, a deal clinched, a loan arranged.

The dress of the prosperous merchant and his family did not differ, in Henry VII's reign, from that of other classes. All men wore long, very tight hose from the waist downwards, with a shirt, a short doublet (like a waistcoat) and a cape or a long cloak. Wealthier men might perhaps have their capes or cloaks furred. Hair was worn long, often to the shoulders, and a small flat cap, sometimes with a feather in it, was perched on top of their heads. In the absence of buttons, the doublet was tied to the hose by lace tags called points. Shoes in an earlier period had become absurdly long and pointed, making walking difficult, but by the start of the Tudor period a much more sensible and practical half-length boot was fashionable. Most men were clean-shaven, like Henry himself.

Generally speaking, there is an absence of show about male costume in the early years of the Tudors. Later in the 16th century, dress became much more elaborate and colourful, rings and earrings were profusely employed and a courtier like Sir Walter Raleigh almost literally carried a fortune about with him in his clothes and jewels. Even the women refrained from undue extravagance in Henry VII's reign; their dresses were very long, brushing the ground at front and back, with a simple girdle at the waist, long sleeves very wide, and head-dresses which, like the hair of their menfolk, came down to their shoulders. There is very little difference in female fashions from those of earlier periods at the start of Henry's reign, though changes to a more elaborate costume are to be observed before his death in 1509

There were only two main meals in early Tudor England, dinner at 10 a.m. and supper at 5 p.m. Naturally these two meals were large ones and there was a great emphasis upon meat; even the peasants ate more meat than their continental counterparts and this was taken by foreign observers to be a sign of England's comparative prosperity. Curious and exotic dishes appeared at the tables of the rich, peacocks, boars' heads and swans among them. Since deer were very numerous and were hunted on a large scale, venison was a frequent meat course. Mutton and beef were of very poor quality by comparison with more modern times, because the proper breeding of sheep and cattle was not then understood and the beasts tended to be thin and their meat lacking in flavour. Also the lack of winter fodder for cattle meant that only a percentage of the animals could be kept alive, so many were slaughtered in the autumn, their meat being preserved by salting. For over half the year, therefore, salted meat had to be eaten and it was to relieve the monotony of this diet that spices were in such great demand, pepper, cloves, nutmeg, cinammon and many others. English herbs were also in great demand and every housewife was familiar with those that grew wild in the fields or hedgerows. Pastry served as a case for meat or as the basis of elaborate sweets, triumphs of culinary skill, which adorned the tables of the wealthy. The potato was unknown and surprisingly little use was made of other vegetables, though fruit, including home-grown grapes, was popular. Beer was easily the commonest drink, for tea and coffee did not appear until the 17th century and wine had to be imported from France or Spain. Women and children drank beer for no one in their senses would drink water unless it came from a very pure spring or well. To drink river water was to court death since filtration was unheard-of.

At mealtimes everyone, including guests, used their own knives, carried in a sheath fixed to the girdle, to cut up the food which was conveyed to the mouth in the fingers. Forks had been in use (with only two prongs) since the middle of the 15th century, but they were not employed as they are to-day. There were neither napkins nor handkerchiefs and the nose was blown by hand; politeness demanded that the hand used was not the one which carried food to the mouth! At the end of the meal in better-class households a bowl of scented water and a hand towel was offered to the eaters for the washing of hands, a necessary ablution after the consumption of some twenty courses. The remains of these vast meals went first to the servants—very numerous in a noble household—and then to the beggars who waited patiently at the gates for the crumbs from the rich man's table. Warwick the Kingmaker is said to have fed five hundred guests on occasions and probably even more servants as well as a horde of the wretched poor.

The peasant and the humble artisan in the towns, of course,

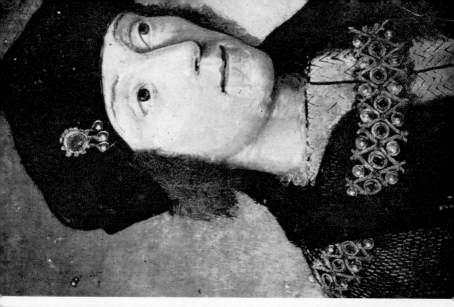

Top: Henry VII as a young man. *Museum Calvet, Avignon.*

Above: Death mask of Henry VII, from the effigy carried in his funeral procession. Photo by *Eric de Mare*

ELIZABETHA · VXOR
HENRICI · VII ·

Elizabeth of York, daughter of Edward IV and wife of Henry VII. *National Portrait Gallery*

Page from the Household Accounts of Henry VII with each item initialled by the king. *Public Record Office (E.101/413/2/2)*

MASTER BRAY. 27 Aug. Item received of Master Bray by thandes of William Cope of the reveneuz of thisle of Wight due at Ester last passed, £108 H.R.
MASTER BRAY. 28 Aug. Item received of Master Bray by thandes of William Coope upon a warrant for gernisshing of the Kinges salades, shapewez and other, £1382.4.3. H.R.
THABBOT OF REDING. 29 Aug. Item received of thabbot of Reding, £133.6.8 H.R.
THOMAS DAVERS. 30 Aug. Item received of Thomas Davers, £40 H.R.
THE LUMBARDEZ. 6 Sept. Item received of the Lumbardez for a licence for the bying of woll, £100 H.R.
Partial sum: £1,763.11s. (Sallets and Chapeaux refer to types of helmet. The variants 'Cope' & 'Coope' are typical of Tudor spelling, and there is an error of 1d. in the addition.)

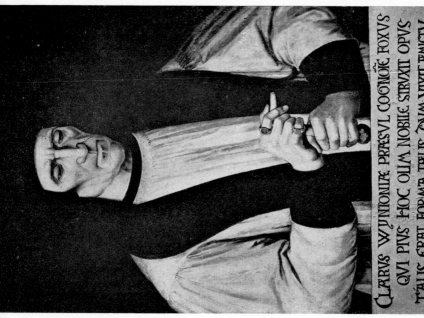

Top: Cardinal Fox, Bishop of Winchester, one of Henry VII's most able servants. By kind permission of the *President, Corpus Christi, Oxford*

Above: A 15th-century street.

fed much less lavishly. Their bread was made of coarser flour and was the staple item of their diet but some meat, as has been said, found its way to their tables, eggs were eaten and sometimes bacon if a few pigs were kept. Dull and monotonous their food must certainly have been, but it was probably more nutritious and appetising than that eaten by the swarming slum dwellers of 19th-century Britain.

The houses of even the wealthiest would seem unbearably uncomfortable to us. There was almost no glass for corridors and landings—it was too expensive even for windows in poorer peoples' dwellings—and the draughts must have been formidable. Furniture was ample enough and included a very large wooden dining table, an equally huge sideboard, chairs often elaborately carved, and roomy four-poster beds. But there were very few carpets and floors still tended to be covered by rushes which were all too rarely renewed and which harboured all sorts of rubbish and dirt. Tapestries took off some of the cold bareness of the walls though these again were luxuries only to be seen in the mansions of the rich. While brick was steadily replacing stone in these mansions, wood and mud were often the materials used in the peasant's cottage. Wood rather than the scarce coal was used for fires and logs sizzled merrily in the enormous fireplaces of the larger houses; the smoke, which in earlier days had escaped via the glassless windows or the doors, now went up chimneys.

There is no doubt that the men and women of this period were extremely tough; in an age when child mortality was appallingly high (Henry VII himself lost two sons in their teens) only the very sturdiest survived. Diseases which to us are trivial, like measles, were killers then—and how many must have perished from appendicitis, the cause of which was quite unknown? If an operation was performed it was done without anaesthetics and with unsterilised instruments, so that shock and blood poisoning must often have proved fatal. In the very first months of Henry's reign, a new and terrible disease appeared in England. This was the 'sweating sickness', a deadly infection in some respects akin to the plague, the 'black death', which was a frequent visitor. Medicine was utterly primitive, relying upon copious bleedings and extraordinary remedies involving the swallowing of nauseating brews. It is a marvel that anyone was ever cured by the doctors at all!

Because death so often came when people were in the prime of life, they tended to start their education and careers much earlier than we do to-day, and they married much sooner so that it was not uncommon for a girl to be a mother at fifteen and a boy to have completed his university studies at the same age. It follows that they aged much more rapidly so that a man of sixty would be considered very old indeed. Henry VII was only fifty-two at his death (his wife Elizabeth was even younger) and Henry VIII, a splendid, athletic man in his twenties, was an enormously stout, disease-ridden figure when he died at the age of fifty-five. It must not be thought, however, that life was all squalor and misery under the perpetual shadow of imminent death. Our early Tudor ancestors knew well enough how to enjoy themselves. The poor, it is true, had little leisure; in 1495 an Act of Parliament ordered that 'between the midst of the month of May and the midst of the month of September every artificer and labourer be at his work before five in the morning and that he depart not from his work till between seven and eight of the evening'. In this long day he had half an hour for his breakfast and an hour and a half for his midday dinner—the breakfast being merely a slice of bread and a pot of ale. But there were Sundays, and twenty-four holidays in the year, usually saints' days and including May Day when the coming of spring was celebrated as it had been for centuries all over Europe. There was then dancing round the maypole, there was jumping and wrestling, perhaps a wandering minstrel or conjurer or acrobat willing to entertain in exchange for a night's food and lodging or a few pence. Football was a popular sport, immensely rough and almost without rules, with teams containing all the able-bodied men of the village, some of whom would suffer broken bones before nightfall terminated the game. Football was officially discouraged since it interfered with archery practice, but it was played just the same, as was golf in Scotland, though not yet in England. The upper classes played cards, which had first appeared in England towards the end of the 15th century, chess, bowls and tennis, gambled on dice and enjoyed such brutal sports as bear-baiting and cock-fighting. Not by any means the least popular of amusements were executions and public whippings for the cruelty of the age was not confined to animals but extended to men and women. More civilized and gentle was the English love of music; an educated man was expected to be able to sing and to play an instrument and in Tudor times when awaiting their turn at the barbers, men would entertain with a tune on the virginals or with a song. Henry VIII was a performer and composer of distinction, though there is no evidence to suggest that his stricter father was similarly gifted. Henry VIII also was able to enjoy a wrestling bout with Francis I of France when they met at the famous Field of the Cloth of Gold. He jousted as well, a pastime still popular among the gentry though much less dangerous to life and limb than it had been in the great tourneys of medieval times.

Women were naturally debarred from active participation in the masculine sports, but this did not mean that they led cloistered lives. They enjoyed the sport of hawking, rode in the hunt, danced, played cards, diced, sang.

19

It was essential that most amusements should be 'home-made' for travel was uncomfortable, difficult and dangerous. In London the river provided the easiest means of transport between the city and Westminster—the business and government areas then as now, but not linked by continuous streets of shops and houses. Henry VII lived at Westminster when he was in London (he was also fond of his fine palace at Richmond where in fact he died), parliament met there, Westminster Hall was the scene of trials and court cases and the great Abbey of Westminster, founded by Edward the Confessor, rose proudly above the smaller buildings clustered round it. To the Abbey Henry added the splendid chapel which bears his name and his tomb. Near the Abbey was the printing press of William Caxton, established in 1477, the first of its kind in England for the invention of printing had taken place in Germany only twenty-seven years before.

Travel in London, with its invaluable river, was one thing, travel outside the capital quite another matter. The roads were few and far between and very rough, often little more than tracks cutting through the huge fields as yet unenclosed by walls, hedges and ditches. There were really no towns as we understand the word, for only three places, Norwich, York, and Bristol had as many as 20,000 inhabitants. Many peasants were born, lived their entire lives and died in the same tiny village, perhaps leaving it on very rare occasions for a brief visit to the market-town a few miles away. There was certainly very little inducement to venture upon the roads unless the journey was absolutely essential, for they were infested by robbers and vagabonds, the 'masterless men', who were to prove a continual problem to Tudor monarchs. Some of these were retainers, whose lords had been killed or impoverished in the Wars of the Roses or who had been forced to dismiss their men by the Acts of Livery and Maintenance; some had been wounded or had broken down in health and could in consequence find no employment and so took to a life of begging or crime or both. To control them and bring them to justice for their crimes there existed only the parish constables, who were supposed to be able to call out honest men to help them to catch a criminal. Shakespeare in *Much Ado About Nothing* has left a humorous picture of Dogberry, one such constable. Here he is briefing his watchmen on their duties:

'If you meet a thief you may suspect him, by virtue of your office, to be no true man; and for such kind of men, the less you meddle or make with them, the more is for your honesty'. The Second Watchman naively enquires: 'If we know him to be a thief, shall we not lay hands upon him?' Dogberry has a ready answer to this: 'The most peaceable way for you, if you do take a thief, is to let him show himself what he is, and steal out of your company'.

Dogberry, perhaps, should not be taken too seriously, though there is an example of behaviour not unlike his much later in the 16th century when some plotters against Elizabeth were being sought, but it is quite clear that criminals could expect at least a fair run for their money if not absolute immunity from punishment.

Disease rampant, life rough and brutal, communications bad, villains in plenty—and yet England was a land of great potential wealth and prosperity. Its people longed for firm and stable government, an end to the disorders and turmoils of the past decades. For them a monarch who was strong and efficient was an absolute necessity, and such a one could count upon their loyal support. Henry VII, by establishing his dynasty upon the throne, was to lay the sturdy foundations upon which his successors could build, but the establishment of that rule was to take time and many perils had to be surmounted before it was achieved.

2

THE THRONE SECURE

The genealogical table on the opposite page illustrates the position of the House of York in 1485. The existence of the daughters of Edward IV and of his nephew, Edward, Earl of Warwick, together with the mystery surrounding the disappearance of his two sons, the 'Princes in the Tower', were to give many opportunities for Yorkist risings and plots against Henry VII. Even to-day there are those who hold that Edward V and Richard, Duke of York were still alive in 1485 and that they were not murdered by their uncle Richard III but on the orders of Henry VII who, it is suggested, found them still in the Tower when he reached London after Bosworth. This theory finds its most interesting expression in a remarkable novel by Josephine Tey called *Daughter of Time*, but it must be said that no serious historians subscribe to the ingenious ideas put forward there and we may therefore assume that the young king and his brother had been put out of the way by Richard III, probably in 1483. Even so, there were Yorkist rivals enough.

Henry very quickly made an attempt to unite the Houses of York and Lancaster by marrying Elizabeth, eldest daughter of Edward IV. Unlike most royal marriages undertaken for political purposes, the match proved to be a happy one and Elizabeth's death in 1503 was sincerely mourned by her husband and his Court. Her younger sisters were married off to loyal but comparatively humble supporters of the king so that no trouble came from them. It was from Edward IV's

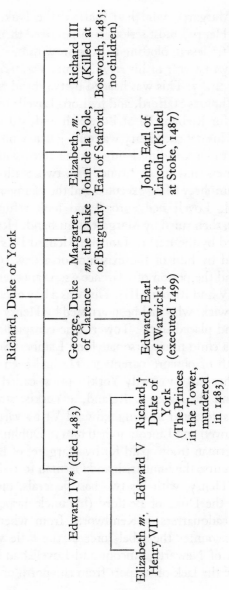

THE HOUSE OF YORK

Richard, Duke of York

Edward IV* (died 1483)
George, Duke of Clarence
Margaret, m. the Duke of Burgundy
Elizabeth, m. John de la Pole, Earl of Stafford
Richard III (Killed at Bosworth, 1485; no children)

Edward, Earl of Warwick‡ (executed 1499)
John, Earl of Lincoln (Killed at Stoke, 1487)

Elizabeth m. Henry VII
Edward V
Richard,† Duke of York (The Princes in the Tower, murdered in 1483)

* Edward IV had four other daughters in addition to Elizabeth
† Impersonated by Perkin Warbeck
‡ Impersonated by Lambert Simnel

23

fiery sister Margaret, who had married the Duke of Burgundy, that Henry's most serious rivals derived their support
and she was tireless in plotting to overthrow him.

In the very first year of his reign, Henry was faced with a
Yorkist conspiracy. This was headed by two brothers, Humphrey and Thomas Stafford, and by Lord Lovell; these three
had fought for Richard III at Bosworth and had gone into
hiding after his defeat. Henry was on a journey north when
he heard of the impending rising and he acted with charac-
teristic firmness and promptitude. The two Staffords were
arrested, Humphrey being executed and the younger Thomas
spared, while Lovell fled abroad and took refuge in the
Netherlands, then ruled by Margaret's husband. Here he was
shortly joined by the Earl of Lincoln, Richard III's nephew,
and was told by him of the existence of a new conspiracy
centred round the person of Clarence's son (another nephew
of Edward IV and Richard III). This was a boy of eleven, the
Earl of Warwick, who had been arrested by Henry VII after
Bosworth and placed in the Tower. The conspirators, however, found a child to impersonate him, Lambert Simnel, an
Oxford youth of obscure parentage. He had been carefully
coached in his part by a wily Yorkist priest called William
Symonds, and then sent to Ireland, a Yorkist stronghold.
Here he was accepted as King Edward VI by various Irish
chieftains. Lovell and Lincoln joined him in Dublin with two
thousand German troops paid for by Margaret of Burgundy
and in due course the joint Irish and German force landed in
Lancashire. Henry, with his two best generals, the Earl of
Oxford and the Duke of Bedford (his uncle Jasper), established his headquarters at Kenilworth from where he ad-
vanced to encounter the rebel force at the little village of
Stoke, south of Newark. Lincoln and Lovell had been disappointed by the lack of support from the north of England

(once an area strong for the Yorkist cause) but they still had eight thousand men and boldly attacked the royal army. After a tough struggle, the rebels were defeated; Lincoln was killed in the battle and Lovell probably drowned in the Trent as he fled from the field; Symonds and Simnel were captured, the priest being condemned to life imprisonment. Simnel, who had been simply the dupe of ambitious men, was found a post in the royal kitchens from which in time he was promoted to be one of the royal falconers. When some of the Irish chiefs who had supported the rising had made their humble submission and were being feasted by Henry in 1489, the king had their wine served to them by Simnel whom they had once acclaimed as their rightful sovereign!

Henry, as always, showed mercy to the rank and file of the rebel army but fined the surviving leaders heavily. They had to pay part of the sum demanded from them immediately while the balance was held as a threat over their heads as a surety for future good behaviour. A competent servant of Henry's, Sir Richard Edgecombe, was sent to Ireland to bring about the surrender of the Irish chiefs who had supported Simnel; he did his job well, for the next pretender received nothing like the help that the Irish had given to Simnel.

This next pretender was to become an even greater threat to the king than Simnel had been. He was a youth called Perkin Warbeck, who was probably the son of a Frenchman of the town of Tournai; this youth was employed by a Breton cloth merchant, Pregent Meno, who took him to Cork in 1491 and dressed him splendidly as a walking advertisement for his wares. Warbeck was handsome and carried himself well and the natives of Cork persuaded him to impersonate Richard, Duke of York, the younger of the Princes in the Tower. There seems little doubt that the scheming hand of Margaret of Burgundy was behind this imposture and, though the Irish chiefs—once bitten, twice shy—gave him little support, Perkin was received at the Burgundian court where Margaret readily acknowledged him as her nephew. While he was thus enjoying life at his 'aunt's' court, Henry struck at traitors nearer home. In 1494 a group of prominent plotters were arrested in London and some of them were executed; early in the following year Sir William Stanley, who had fought with Henry at Bosworth and had actually placed Richard's crown on Henry's head after the battle, was arrested and beheaded. He had been given the important post of Lord Chamberlain in 1485 and was thought to be the richest man in England apart from the king, but these facts had not prevented him from plotting against his master.

In July 1495 Warbeck appeared off the Kent coast and some of his followers landed to try to raise support. The arrests and executions of the previous year had, however, destroyed the leaders of the conspiracy in England and the Kentish peasants would not rise in favour of Warbeck, who sailed away to Ireland. Here he failed to capture the port of Waterford and so moved on to Scotland where he enjoyed better fortune. James IV, the Scottish king, received him well, realizing that here was a heaven-sent opportunity to embarrass the English king. Clothes and money were given to the pretender and he was married to Lady Catherine Gordon, a distant relation of James. Late in 1496 the Scots invaded England but utterly failed to secure any success. In July 1497 James sent Warbeck out of his kingdom, though he continued his war with Henry. Warbeck revisited Ireland but received little assistance there, and then journeyed to Cornwall hoping to benefit from recent events in that county.

When the Scots invaded England, Henry had persuaded Parliament to grant him taxation so that troops could be raised to meet the threat from the north. The Cornishmen resented being made to pay money to defend counties at the other end of England and rose in rebellion under the leadership of a lawyer, Thomas Flamank, and a blacksmith, Michael Joseph. Marching eastwards, the rebels were joined at Wells by Baron Audley, at one time a loyal Lancastrian. They then brushed aside a tiny royalist force near Guildford and decided to make for Kent, hoping to recruit further support in that county. In this, they were utterly disappointed by the obstinate loyalty of the people of that county, but their number was still the high one of 15,000 and in June 1497 they faced a royal army of 25,000 at Blackheath. The Cornishmen were unable to cope with the superior discipline and numbers of the royal army and were heavily defeated. Only the three leaders were executed after the battle, but this royal mercy did not achieve its object for Warbeck found several hundred supporters when he reached Cornwall in September. He tried to take Exeter but failed miserably and was captured at Beaulieu in Hampshire. He was brought to London and made to confess in public that he was an impostor. Henry treated him kindly, keeping him only in a loose imprisonment until he tried to escape from this, when he was placed under stricter arrest in the Tower. Again he tried to escape and was therefore executed in 1499. With him suffered the hapless Earl of Warwick who had been a captive for fourteen years and was, not surprisingly, feeble in mind and body.

With the deaths of Warbeck and Warwick, Henry could at last consider himself safe upon his throne and only the ineffectual plotting of the Earl of Suffolk disturbed his last years.

Behind all these plots and risings lurked the sinister figures of the 'over-mighty subjects', the powerful barons who had survived the Wars of the Roses and who continued to keep large numbers of servants who owed obedience to their masters rather than to the king. They wore the livery or uniform of their lords and the latter 'maintained' them, that is to say supported them by bribery or force if they faced criminal charges in the law courts. In 1487 Parliament passed the Act of Livery and Maintenance which was intended to curtail the number of retainers employed by the nobles. Enforcement of this Act proved difficult and other similar acts were passed by later parliaments. The famous story of John de Vere, Earl of Oxford, illustrates this point : he had lavishly entertained the king at his country house and when the time came for Henry to leave the Earl drew up his retainers, all in livery, as a guard of honour. The king, it is said, thanked the Earl for his hospitality but added that he could not allow his laws to be broken so blatantly and the Earl was in consequence very heavily fined.

Henry had revived and strengthened a former royal law court to enforce Livery and Maintenance and to discipline his powerful subjects. This Court took its name from the room in the palace of Westminster in which it met—the Star Chamber. The judges in it were Privy Councillors and there was no jury to be bribed and intimidated. It could not sentence men to death, but it could—and did—impose heavy fines; above all, it was a court in which poor and humble men could hope to win actions against the mightiest men in the kingdom. An episode in 1503 illustrates the function of Star Chamber and also the unruly behaviour of Englishmen of this period. There was a monastery near Oxford at a place called Eynsham. The Abbot had a dispute with a local knight, Sir Robert Harcourt, about fishing rights. In the February of 1503 one of the monks, called Roger Wallingford, and a monastic servant named Christopher took a boat to an island in the middle of the Thames and went ashore to gather stones with which to weight their fishing nets. John Walsh, one of Harcourt's servants, thereupon rowed the boat away 'intending to have destroyed them and so left them there to perish, for it was cold weather and frost'. Luckily for Roger and Christopher, their cries for help were heard and they were rescued from their unpleasant plight, but this was by no means the end of the affair. A day or so later, Walsh rowed his own boat into the private stream running through the monastic orchard; two of the monks thereupon seized the boat and locked it to a tree. Walsh struck one of them and the other 'perceiving the malicious disposition of the said John' very sensibly ran away with Walsh in hot pursuit. Sir Robert next sent an armed force to recapture his boat and actually laid siege to the monastery. When this siege proved unsuccessful, he held a court at Henley and accused the monks of riot and felony. 'If the jury be not returned after his mind, he stoppeth them with threatening and other means'. Small wonder that the Abbot, despairing of obtaining justice in such a court, appealed to the Star Chamber. The result of his appeal is not known, but it is probable that the riotous activities of Sir Robert and his retainers were sharply curbed.

Henry possessed one very valuable weapon in his struggles with his over-mighty subjects: he had the only siege train in England and could threaten his subjects' castles with its elaborate and effective weapons which included a number of cannon. Against these even the strongest walls would be defenceless and as few lords were willing to see their homes knocked down about their ears the mere threat of the siege train was sufficient and there is no evidence that Henry ever had to use it. It was, of course, a highly expensive affair and the fact that Henry possessed it illustrates the success of his financial policy.

'What he minded, he compassed.' Henry realized that money meant power and was determined to build up a fortune which would make him the richest—and therefore the

most powerful—man in England. This he had to accomplish
without recourse to frequent parliamentary taxation for this
would result in unpopularity and possibly rebellion. Fortun-
ately for the king there were numerous other sources of
improvement for the royal finances. Of these, four rank as the
most important :

(i) Crown lands.
(ii) The profits of justice, fines imposed in the law courts.
(iii) Customs duties.
(iv) Feudal dues.

A king of England held very extensive lands and was indeed the greatest landowner in the country with the exception
of the Church. During the Wars of the Roses, however, much
Crown land had been lost and the rents from that which remained had been irregularly and inefficiently collected. A
monarch who was engaged in civil war or who was in prison
or exile obviously could not supervise the collection of the
sums due to him or prevent his enemies from seizing the royal
estates in areas of the country which they controlled. Like the
born man of business that he was, Henry set out to remedy
this state of affairs. He persuaded his first parliament to date
his reign from the day *before* the Battle of Bosworth and thus
made all those who had fought there for Richard III traitors
though they were no such thing for they had been fighting for
their lawful king. Now when a man was convicted of treason
all his lands and possessions were confiscated by the crown
though the king might, out of the kindness of his heart,
permit the traitor's wife and family to retain just enough to
keep themselves alive. The confiscations of the estates of those
who had fought for Richard III, together with those suffered
by later rebels and traitors, greatly increased the royal property
and Henry saw to it that his rents, when he let out his land,

were promptly and fully collected. So, whereas in the first year of his reign only £4,000 came from Crown property, at the time of his death in 1509 the figure had risen to no less than £30,000.

The profits of justice amounted to a considerable sum as Star Chamber and other courts imposed heavy fines upon wealthy offenders. We have no means of knowing what Henry's annual income was from this source, especially as many fines were not paid immediately but in instalments, but the sum involved cannot have been an insignificant one for Bacon, in one of his rare criticisms of the king, admits that towards the end of his reign his courts 'meddled somewhat too much with meum and tuum', implying that Henry was not above tampering with the course of justice if he stood to gain financially by doing so.

Edward IV had not hesitated to indulge in trading ventures and had made some handsome profits in the process. Henry VII followed his predecessor's example in this. In 1505-6 he actually made £15,000 from a deal in alum and he also dabbled successfully in the wool trade with Flanders. Profit from these activities, however, was less than that derived from the customs duties which were bringing in nearly £40,000 a year to the Treasury by the end of the reign. Prominent among these customs duties was tunnage and poundage, a levy upon imports. Tunnage applied to imports of wine which came to England in large barrels or tuns. It will be seen later in this book how skilfully Henry made trade treaties with other countries to the great profit of himself and his subjects. It is certain that his encouragement of law and order in the realm gave every inducement to its merchants to increase their trading activities.

Feudal dues had long been a fruitful source of royal income. These were payments which the king was entitled to collect from his landowning subjects. They were obliged to pay him money on the occasion of the marriage of their daughters and the knighting of their sons and to supply him with horses and carts (or a sum of money in their place) when he set out with his court upon a progress round his country. More unpopular even than these dues were wardships: when a landowner died leaving a child of under legal age to inherit his estates, the king was entitled to assume wardship (guardianship) of that child until he or she came of age and to enjoy the profits of the estate. As early death was commonplace in this period of history there were numerous orphans and the king could be guardian over many profitable estates. Henry did not hesitate to ask parliament for money when a suitable excuse existed as, for example, when the threat of Lambert Simnel or Perkin Warbeck was at its height. This, as has been seen, provoked a rebellion in Cornwall for the people living in that county did not see why they should be called upon to pay taxes to preserve the northern counties from a Scottish invasion, but parliament itself was usually quite willing to grant the king money in an emergency and the people, though no doubt they grumbled, paid. In 1491, when Henry was contemplating an invasion of France, he summoned a parliament to grant him money with which to conduct the campaign, and Bacon says that the king himself addressed that parliament to explain his reasons for going to war and to invite their financial support—which was immediately forthcoming. This episode, incidentally, makes clear the role of parliament in the government of the time. Its members were not expected to discuss, still less to criticize, the royal policy but simply to have it explained to them so that they might inform their constituents of the need for taxation and make the necessary arrangements for its collection. Henry would have been horrified at the idea of M.P.s in the Com-

Plan of London, circa 1553. This map, which post-dates the reign of Henry VII by about forty years, shows the various watergates and wharves on the Thames, London Bridge and the city of Westminster, linked to the city of London by only one street with houses. It will be noted that most of London was to the east of St. Paul's. Two circular theatres on the Southwark bank would not have been built in Henry VII's reign. *The London Topographical Society*

Top: A friar preaching outside a church.

Above: The family of Sir Thomas More (centre) by Hans Holbein, court painter to Henry VIII. *The Hon. R. D. G. Winn, M.C.*

Left: The farmyard of a country house in the mid-15th century.

Above: Shepherds with their dogs—and various curious animals and birds.

Top: The superb fan-vaulting in Henry VII's Chapel in Westminster Abbey.

Above: The tomb of Henry VII and his queen in Westminster Abbey. This was the work of the Italian artist, Torregiani. Pictures—*Church Information Office*

mons debating royal policy, as they were to do with such freedom in a later period of history.

Having obtained funds from his loyal subjects, Henry duly invaded France in 1492 with an army of 14,000 men. Very quickly the French king sued for peace and a treaty was accordingly signed at Etaples. By it, Charles VIII promised to pay Henry a large annual sum so that the wily English king had obtained money from his people to wage a war and money from his opponent to stop doing so—and all this after a campaign lasting exactly three weeks! His policy here was very similar to that of Edward IV who had invaded France in 1471 and then allowed himself to be bought off by the Treaty of Pécquigny.

In these various ways, Henry built up his fortune. As early as 1499, the Spanish ambassador wrote 'his riches increase every day. I think that he has no equal in this respect'. He goes on to say 'all his servants possess a wonderful dexterity in getting other peoples' money'—and this was written before Empson and Dudley, royal servants, became notorious in the closing years of the reign for their financial skill exercised upon the king's behalf. Empson and Dudley were not, as is sometimes stated, tax collectors, for parliament met only once in the last nine years and therefore no taxation could have been granted in most of those years. It was in the collection of royal fines and feudal dues that Empson and Dudley excelled and made themselves so widely hated in the process that on his accession Henry VIII had them both executed on trumped-up charges, a typical gesture of ingratitude to men who had toiled to amass his father's fortune which he was to dissipate with remarkable speed.

This fortune is thought to have been between £1½ and £2 million, but it is really impossible to assess the figure at all accurately for much of it was not in cash but in jewels, plate, silks and tapestries. It is known that Henry spent over £100,000 on jewellery alone between 1491 and 1503 and no doubt many of the purchases made then were left to his son.

There was nothing new about the first Tudor's financial policy for he imposed no fresh taxes and devised no novel means of raising money. As with his system of government, he simply took the existing methods and made them work, employing a number of loyal and capable servants to assist him and keeping a very close personal check upon his income and expenditure. No item was too trivial to escape the king's all-seeing eye, and he was hard upon officials whom he found to be idle or dishonest. He was a remarkably hard worker himself and he expected equally hard work from his underlings. So he was the last English king to 'live of his own' and to bequeath a fortune to his heir. His son Henry VIII, in the pride and splendour of his youth, all too rapidly spent his father's bequest, and very soon afterwards England, in common with most European countries, was affected by a serious rise in prices. So there was no escape for the English monarchy from the problems of shortage of money, a shortage which could only be remedied by appeals to parliament for increased taxation. This naturally strengthened the power of that body until, in the late seventeenth century, it took over control of the country's finances and reduced the king to the position of a paid servant of the state.

Happily for Henry VII these developments cast no shadows over his reign. He was able to amass his fortune with the vital assistance of his hand-picked servants. Very prominent among these was Cardinal Morton, Archbishop of Canterbury from 1486 until his death in 1500. Morton had a peculiar genius for obtaining money for his king, a genius which has given rise to the story of Morton's Fork. The wily clergyman, so the tale goes, would approach a man who lived an extravagant life

34

and point out that he could obviously afford to make the king a generous 'loan'. To someone who led an austere or miserly existence, Morton would say that he must have saved plenty of money and could therefore also afford to give freely!

Morton is an excellent example of the clergyman-politician-civil servant. Another was Fox, Bishop of Winchester, an extremely able man who was entrusted with the negotiation of an important trade treaty in 1496. Fox had no time to attend to his episcopal duties in Henry's reign, but six years after the king's death he retired from court to his diocese and there devoted himself to clerical activities.

Apart from the small group of nobles on his Council, men such as his uncle Jasper whom Henry made Duke of Bedford, and de Vere, the Earl of Oxford, Henry enjoyed the help of a remarkable body of men who were active in the administration of the kingdom and of its finances. Empson and Dudley have already been mentioned; less unpopular were Bray, Belknap, Poynings and Edgecombe, to name but a few. These men were of comparatively humble origins, nor did they rise high in the peerage as a reward for their services. Henry VII was very sparing in his distribution of high honours, and knighthoods were as much as these men could hope to obtain. Yet they were vital cogs in the machine, devoted men, hard workers, loyal and honest. The extraordinary knack possessed by the Tudors of choosing good men to serve them is as apparent in the reign of the first as it is in the reign of Elizabeth, the last. The Council of Henry VII's time kept virtually no records, so we do not know how much of the king's policy was of his own making and how much resulted from the advice of his councillors. We can be sure, however, that nothing was decided or carried out without the royal consent and it may be that Henry originated everything and left the carrying out of his decisions to his ministers.

The Council was a large, unwieldy body with no fixed membership: Henry's middle-class councillors provided a solid core—the professionals among the amateurs. It is unfortunate that so little is known of their individual contributions for the official posts they occupied meant very little; Sir Reginald Bray, for instance, held the minor position of chancellor of the Duchy of Lancaster, but was, in fact, one of the most important and capable of Henry's administrators. Unlike the notorious Dudley and Empson, Bray refrained from lining his own pockets and thus avoided the hatred which they—not undeservedly—evoked.

The men on the Council relied for the carrying-out of their instructions upon a body of men whose importance greatly increased during Henry VII's reign and continued to increase throughout the Tudor period. These were the Justices of the Peace, local gentlemen of wealth and standing who acted as the unpaid 'Tudor maids-of-all-work'. The Council appointed them on a year-to-year basis and did not hesitate to shower advice, praise and blame upon them. Generally speaking they were loyal and competent, but they were not averse to ignoring orders or instructions from the Council of which they did not approve or which conflicted with their own interests. No Tudor government, however efficient, could rely upon absolute and immediate enforcement of its laws. But even with these reservations in mind, the employment of the J.P.s was a remarkably successful move on the part of Henry VII and his successors. It would not have been so successful, of course, had not the Tudors managed to establish their control over the country so effectively and had they not been so well served by their councillors. Strong *central* government alone could ensure strong local government.

The existence of this essential strong central government in Tudor England has led some people to call the Tudor monarchs despots or tyrants. Nowadays we are all too familiar with tyranny as a method of governing states and we know that two of the essentials for a tyranny are a powerful police force and a large, obedient army. The Tudors had neither of these : the absence of a competent police force has already been mentioned but the fact that the Tudors had no regular standing army has not. It is this which largely accounts for the successes gained by rebels in the 16th century during the early weeks of their risings. When Henry VII, for instance, wanted to collect an army, he could only do so by using a slow and complicated machinery which involved the Lords Lieutenant of the counties (in those times very important men) and the Justices of the Peace. These officials were instructed to raise a certain number of soldiers from their areas, arm them and provide them with adequate clothing—there were no military uniforms then—and send them to an appointed rendezvous by an appointed date.

Shakespeare, once again, provides us with an idea of how this curious system worked in the famous scene in *Henry IV*, Part II, where Sir John Falstaff, who has been placed in command of some troops yet to be mustered, visits Shallow and Silence, two elderly J.P.s to see what men they have summoned for service :

Falstaff. Have you provided me here half a dozen sufficient men?

Shallow. Marry, have we, sir. Will you sit?

Falstaff. Let me see them, I beseech you.

Shallow. Where's the roll? Where's the roll? Where's the roll? Let me see, let me see, let me see. So, so, so, so, so, so, so : yea, marry, sir : Ralph Mouldy! Let them appear as I call; let them do so, let them do so. Let me see; Where is Mouldy?

Mouldy (a ragged, tattered scarecrow). Here, an't please you.

Falstaff. Is thy name Mouldy?

Mouldy. Yea, an't please you.

Falstaff. Tis the more time thou wert used.

When Falstaff has eventually made his selection from the ill-assorted bunch presented to him as possible soldiers, he chooses his six, then accepts bribes from some of them to be excused from serving! As with the constable Dogberry referred to earlier, we need not assume that all recruits were of this calibre nor that all captains were as dishonest as Falstaff, but Shakespeare was obviously well aware that the system of recruiting still employed in his day left a good deal to be desired.

One military 'force' Henry VII did create. On the day of his coronation, October 30th, 1485, he ordered the raising of a band of archers, under a captain, to act as the royal body-guard and to be called the yeomen of the guard; these were the forerunners of the 'beefeaters' still to be seen in their picturesque uniforms guarding the Tower of London.

Tyrannies are not maintained by troops levied slowly by cumbersome medieval methods nor by a handful of archers whose number would be insufficient to accompany a modern dictator on a short car journey, and it is a matter for wonder that the Tudors were yet able to establish themselves and to bring stability to a people whom the Venetian ambassador early in Henry's reign described as being more unruly than any in Europe. Henry VII was no warmonger; when he raised armies they were to deal with domestic risings which threatened the very existence of his line. Only very briefly (and profitably) did he engage in foreign wars; he was wise before his time in realizing how costly warfare and the maintenance of large armies had become. It was not that he was cowardly.

Far from it. He was the best soldier in the England of his day and he had the ability to choose good soldiers, like his uncle Jasper and Lord Daubeny. The foreign war in which Henry did become involved is among the subjects of the next chapter.

3

FOREIGN AFFAIRS

At home, Henry devoted all his efforts to the great task of consolidating his rule. In his foreign policy he pursued a similar course, for recognition of the Tudor line by other European countries would obviously be of the utmost value to him.

Europe in 1485 presented a very different picture to the Europe we know today. Russia (or Muscovy as it was generally called) was entirely remote from the rest of the continent, with no religious links or commercial contacts with the other countries. To the south of Russia and sprawling into the Balkans was the Ottoman Empire, the territory of the Mohammedan Turks and their subject peoples. The extensive trade of the Eastern Mediterranean and the Near East lay under their control and they ruled Palestine and the holy places of the Christian faith. To the west of the Ottoman Empire was Italy, a collection of independent states, not a united country. Among these states were the territories of the Pope whose capital was Rome and who controlled a large area of central Italy. South of the Papal States was the kingdom of the Two Sicilies which comprised the island of Sicily and the southern part of the Italian peninsula. North of the Papal states were a large number of powerful, wealthy cities of which

Florence and Venice were outstanding examples. Venice at this time still enjoyed an enormous trade and acted as the distributor of goods from the East to the rest of Europe. These Italian city-states had their own rulers, their own armies, laws and currencies; they made alliances and fought wars and were very shortly to be closely involved in the great struggle that developed between France and the Holy Roman Empire, a struggle in which most of the fighting took place in Italy. This Holy Roman Empire comprised what is today Germany, together with Austria, and its emperor was a member of the House of Hapsburg. His control over Austria, the hereditary possession of his family, was firm enough, but in Germany his position was much weaker. In the first place, he was elected to the post of Emperor by a small group of German princes who themselves ruled over their own territories— Bavaria and Brandenburg, for example. These electoral princes, like the many less important German rulers, owed nominal loyalty to the Emperor but this did not stop them from carrying out their own policies even if these ran counter to his wishes. There were over three hundred states in Germany, some, like the two mentioned above, large and of growing importance, some merely single cities governing perhaps a small area outside the city walls. After 1493, the Emperor was Maximilian whose rule lasted until 1519 and was marked by determined though not wholly successful attempts to assert his power over the German states.

France was developing fast into a major European country. In 1453 the Hundred Years War had ended with the expulsion of England from all her French territories except for the port of Calais. Two capable kings, Louis XI and Charles VIII, had added to the possessions of the French crown partly at the expense of Burgundy whose Duke held extensive lands to the east and north-east. These French kings pursued the same sort of policy at home as did the early Tudors in England, aiming always to increase royal power and to weld the country into a real nation.

Exactly the same process was also going on in Spain and it is because of the activities of the rulers of France, England and Spain that historians refer to this period of European history as the age of the 'new monarchy'. This 'new monarchy' in Spain resulted from the marriage of Ferdinand, king of Aragon, and Isabella, queen of Castile, in 1469. This united the two great Spanish kingdoms, hitherto independent of each other. There remained the conquest of Granada, the southern province ruled by the Moors whose ancestors had once dominated the whole Spanish peninsula, and this final act of unification was completed in the 1490s by 'the most Catholic kings' as Ferdinand and Isabella were called. With the Moslem power in Granada broken, the path was clear for the astonishing development of a united Spain, marked in the first half of the 16th century by the acquisition of a vast Central and Southern American Empire.

The expulsion of the English from the whole of France except for Calais, followed as it was by the internal disruption caused by the Wars of the Roses, had naturally weakened the country's position in European affairs though Edward IV had played a fairly important role in the diplomatic events of his reign. Henry VII was to bring England into close relations with France, Spain, Burgundy and the Holy Roman Empire but not before many complicated events—and some fighting —had taken place.

The first crisis which Henry faced after his accession conerned Brittany, the independent state in north-west France. In 1485 its Duke, Francis II, was an old man in poor health whose death could not be long delayed. He had two daughters but no son. In 1488 France forced a treaty upon the Duke (who died a few weeks later) by which his elder daughter, Anne, would come under French domination. This pleased neither Spain nor England. Henry was in an awkward dilemma. He had established friendly relations with Charles VIII even before he secured the English throne, yet Brittany had been his first place of refuge when he had fled from Wales in his youth, and no doubt he felt that he owed a debt of gratitude to its Duke's daughter. So he attempted to build up a coalition of powers to frustrate French ambitions in Brittany, and Spain was the country whose allegiance he particularly sought. The result was the Treaty of Medina del Campo, signed on March 27th 1489. This treaty was to have very far-reaching effects upon English history : in the first place it laid a firm basis for friendship between the two powers which, with only occasional rifts, lasted for nearly a hundred years; in the second place, it was to be sealed by a marriage between Henry's eldest son Arthur and Catherine, daughter of Ferdinand and Isabella. A further treaty, in 1497, was needed before this marriage was finally agreed upon, and it eventually took place amid great splendour and rejoicing in November 1501. Mercifully hidden in the future were the trials and tribulations which were to be inflicted upon the young bride.

Medina del Campo bound England and Spain to assist Anne of Brittany to preserve her Duchy's independence from France. It was less easy to make an alliance with Maximilian, son and heir of the Holy Roman Emperor, and ruler of Burgundy. With him Henry had not been on good terms, but in February 1489 they agreed to sink their differences in making common cause with Brittany against France.

Unfortunately for Anne, only Henry VII of her supporters made any vigorous efforts on her behalf. In April 1489 an English force of some 6,000 men had landed in Brittany only to find that their attack upon the French king was unsupported by their allies. Maximilian had troubles of his own to contend with, notably a rebellion (aided by France) among his subjects in the Low Countries (Belgium as we know it today). The rebels besieged the town of Dixmude and Maximilian asked Henry for help. This was at once forthcoming: the English king sent an army, ably commanded by Lord Daubeny, and this force saved Dixmude and with it Maximilian's precarious hold over his subjects in the Low Countries. Six weeks later Maximilian repaid Henry for his help by making a treaty with the French king which effectively prevented him from assisting Brittany. Meanwhile, Ferdinand, heavily occupied in his campaigns against the Mohammedans in Granada, had neglected to send assistance also—so the great anti-French coalition had broken up before it had begun to be effective. Now Henry showed the dogged determination which was one of his outstanding characteristics. Painstakingly he re-created his coalition, bringing into it once again the fickle Maximilian and the crafty Ferdinand. Maximilian, a widower, was promised the hand of the Duchess Anne and Ferdinand was persuaded to send a thousand men into Brittany. Yet all this was unavailing for the coalition fell apart almost immediately. Neither the English troops nor the handful of Spaniards in Brittany were able to resist heavy French pressure and Anne, sickened by the strife which was laying waste to her duchy, decided on peace. She repudiated her engagement to Maximilian and accepted instead an offer of marriage from her former enemy, Charles VIII of France. This marriage took place in December 1491 and with it disappeared the last traces of Breton independence. Maximilian calmly accepted the loss of his prospective bride, Ferdinand continued his Granada campaign; only Henry decided to continue the struggle with France. There was more than pride at stake : Anne had promised him financial reward for his help and this had not been paid. Money was therefore obtained from Parliament and an invasion of France was launched. This speedily ended in the favourable Treaty of Etaples (1492) by which Charles VIII agreed to pay England a considerable amount of money and also promised that he would not in any way assist Yorkist pretenders.

From this time on, English relations with Charles VIII and his successor Louis XII were good during Henry VII's reign.

Whenever England and France had been at war, Scotland had been a problem because there was a long-standing alliance between France and Scotland which usually brought the Scots in on France's side. In Shakespeare's *Henry V* there is this passage.

> *Henry V*. We must not only arm to invade the French
> But lay down our proportions to defend
> Against the Scot, who will make road upon us
> With all advantages.

His Archbishop of Canterbury replies that the northern English will be quite capable of looking after themselves against Scottish raiders, but Henry answers:

> We do not mean the coursing snatchers only
> But fear the main intendment of the Scot
> Who hath been still a giddy neighbour to us;
> For you shall read that my great-grandfather
> Never went with his forces into France
> But that the Scot on his unfurnish'd kingdom
> Came pouring, like the tide into a breach.

The 'coursing snatchers' to whom Henry V refers here were the Scottish border lords and their retainers who were all too willing to indulge in cattle-raiding into northern England, nor were the English northern lords averse to similar raids into southern Scotland; indeed these forays were almost as much annual, routine events as the modern soccer and rugger matches between the two countries. John Arden's brilliant play *Armstrong's Last Good-Night* deals with the career of one Scottish border lord who lived in the reign of our Henry VIII. 'The main intendment of the Scots', that is, the might of the whole Scottish army led by its king, was what Henry V and Henry VII had to fear.

James IV of Scotland had not, in fact, been able to interfere when England and France were at war in 1490–92; he had come to the throne in 1488 when only a boy of fifteen and earlier in that year England and Scotland had made a three-years' truce which the young king did not wish to break. In 1495, however, the pretender Perkin Warbeck arrived in Scotland and was well received and in September of the following year James IV invaded England. This expedition was a failure and James soon abandoned Warbeck's cause, though he again invaded England in 1497. The campaign was again brief and was ended by the Truce of Ayton which was to last seven years. In 1502 this truce was confirmed and extended and arrangements were made for a marriage between James IV and Henry's daughter Margaret. The wedding was held in Edinburgh in August 1503, and for the remaining years of Henry's lifetime Anglo-Scottish relations were good. They did not long survive him, for in 1513—when Henry VIII was at war with France—James IV invaded England in strength, only to perish with the flower of his nobility at Flodden. Despite this, the marriage of James and Margaret was destined in time to unite their two countries under one king, James VI of Scotland becoming James I of England in 1603.

Another country which had given help to the pretenders to Henry's throne was Ireland. Unlike Scotland this had the same king as England, but royal power was just as difficult to enforce in Ireland as it was in England. Indeed, the English could only claim to be supreme in a very small area, called the Pale, around Dublin. Beyond the Pale, except in a handful of ports which found trade with England useful, Irish chiefs really ruled though they were supposed to be loyal and obedient subjects of the English crown. Two of the most important of these chiefs, the Earls of Kildare and of Desmond, had been staunch Yorkists, and Kildare had been Lord-Deputy, the king's right-hand man in Ireland. This post he kept at the start of Henry VII's reign but in 1487 he accepted the impostor Lambert Simnel as the rightful king of England. When Simnel's rising collapsed at the Battle of Stoke, Henry sent Sir Richard Edgecombe to Ireland; even Dublin had been disloyal to Henry and Edgecombe at once compelled its citizens to seek forgiveness. But Kildare was too powerful a figure to be removed from his high office and he remained as Lord Deputy after taking an oath of loyalty to Henry upon which Edgecombe insisted. When Warbeck arrived in Ireland four years later Kildare at least offered him no help, though some other Irish chiefs were quick to forget their promises. Kildare was suspected of helping Warbeck and lost his position, after which some fighting took place between him and his enemies. Henry appointed a new Deputy, Lord Gormanston, but soon replaced him by an Englishman, Sir Edward Poynings, one of the king's 'new men'. Poynings went to Ireland late in 1494 with the intention of punishing those who had helped Warbeck, but found that he had first to deal with Kildare who was arrested in February 1495 and sent to England. Kildare's brother at once rebelled, but Poynings, with reinforcements from England, proved too strong for him and so was able to proceed with the vital task of bringing the Irish parliament firmly under English control. This parliament passed the various acts which are collectively called 'Poynings Laws'. Two of these had the desired effect: the Irish parliament in future could make no laws without English consent and all laws passed by English parliaments were to apply to Ireland. Determined attempts were made by this parliament to stamp out the private wars and inter-tribal murders which had been the bane of Ireland for centuries, the Pale was to be defended by the digging of an enormous ditch and Englishmen were to be placed in command of the most important Irish castles. Taxation was to be raised properly so that Ireland would not prove a constant source of embarrassment to the English crown, though this did not always work out as well as had been hoped, for Ireland was a poor country and one in which efficient tax collection was a difficult matter.

In December 1495 Poynings returned to England, his work well done, and after a few months had elapsed his successor was appointed—none other than Kildare. This Earl must have possessed more than his fair share of Irish 'blarney', for he quite charmed Henry; when one of Kildare's numerous enemies said to the king: 'All Ireland cannot rule that gentleman', Henry replied: 'No? Then that gentleman must rule all Ireland.' Before returning to his native country Kildare married a distant relation of Henry's and, once back in power, he proved himself loyal and competent.

So, after many difficulties, Henry proved as successful in Ireland as he was in England. Unfortunately, later English monarchs were less fortunate in their dealings with the Irish, and the island became a problem which no English king or parliament could solve satisfactorily.

While Henry was coping with Scotland and Ireland, the attention of France, Spain and the Empire was taken up by the outbreak of the Italian Wars. While Charles VIII was still king, the French had invaded Northern Italy and had there clashed with Spain. Louis XII renewed this contest as soon as he ascended the French throne in 1498. The warring nations sought the help of England but Henry with great skill kept his country from becoming involved in these costly affairs while remaining on good terms with both France and Spain. He was concerned with building up England's trade. As early as 1490 he had concluded trading agreements with Denmark and Florence and he helped English merchants to play a part in commerce with Venice and with the important group of Baltic merchants who formed the Hanseatic League. In 1496 he sent Cardinal Fox, his Archbishop of Canterbury, to make a treaty with Flanders, centre of the vital wool trade. This trade had lapsed in the years before 1496 with evil results to English prosperity but the Magnus Intercursus, as the agreement was called, restarted it on terms advantageous to both parties. Ten years later Henry attempted the Malus Intercursus which would have revised Magnus Intercursus in favour of the English merchants but this was too one-sided ever to be accepted by the Flemish. Magnus Intercursus was, however, a sufficient achievement in itself and typifies Henry's wise, unspectacular foreign policy. It was not heroic, but it succeeded and at the end of Henry's life England had alliances, strengthened by marriages or marriage alliances with Spain, Scotland and France (whose king was betrothed to Mary, Henry's younger daughter soon after 1509); pretenders to the English throne had found their hopes of foreign aid crumbling away as Henry persuaded his fellow-monarchs that the Tudors were on the throne to stay. Accepted in England, the new dynasty was, by 1509, accepted in Europe.

4

THE ACHIEVEMENTS OF HENRY VII

The last chapter was concerned with wars and rumours of wars, treaties and diplomatic marriages. However, it must not be thought that these were the only matters of importance taking place in the Europe of Henry VII's time. On the contrary things were happening which were to have a significance far greater and more enduring than battles and treaties.

These 'things' make up what is called in history the Renaissance. This is the rebirth of interest in and knowledge of biblical and early Christian writings and also of the literature and art of ancient Rome and ancient Greece. In medieval Europe, scholarship had tended to become very narrow and restricted and we find learned men discussing trivial points of theology with a vigour and ability quite out of proportion to the importance of the subjects. In the 14th century, however, a fresh wind blew down the dusty corridors of schools and universities when great scholars from Byzantium, the capital of the Christian Eastern Empire and the city better known to us as Constantinople or Istanbul, brought to Italy manuscripts of early classical and religious writings. These men with their priceless treasures found a ready welcome in the Italian universities and these became places of pilgrimage for theologians and scholars from all over Europe. In 1453, the Turks captured and sacked Constantinople killing the Christian Emperor; this disaster to Christendom did not start the flow of scholars from east to west but certainly caused some more of them to flee from the doomed city with such manuscripts as they could take with them.

The renewed interest in the Greek and Roman empires meant that artists, particularly architects and sculptors, began to model their works upon those of the men of Athens and Rome who, centuries before, had produced masterpieces. The very wealthy independent cities of Northern Italy such as Florence and Milan had rulers who were generous patrons of the arts and were willing to commission remarkable artists to build and beautify their palaces and churches and the popes themselves were also to be lavish in their encouragement. Thus there is in common use the phrase 'Renaissance art' which describes the particular style of painting, sculpture or architecture which marks this period.

Even more significant, however, was the revival in the study of the Bible made possible by easier access to the new and more authentic editions. Englishmen were among those who took eager advantage of the opportunities thus offered and two or three of them earned outstanding reputations as scholars in Henry VII's reign. In 1487 Thomas Linacre went to Italy where he remained for twelve years studying at Florence and Venice. On his return to England he was appointed tutor to Prince Arthur by the king and he also lectured at Oxford where he had considerable influence over two younger men, John Colet and Thomas More. Linacre was not merely a classical and biblical scholar; he was expert in medicine and not only founded the Royal College of Physicians but bequeathed his money to the encouragement of medical studies at Oxford and Cambridge.

For part of his long stay in Italy, Linacre enjoyed the company of William Grocyn who came back to Oxford in 1492 to lecture on the original Greek text of the New Testament which he rightly considered far more authentic than the Latin translation which had been used almost exclusively for over a thousand years.

Just a year after Grocyn returned from Italy, John Colet set out for an extensive tour of France and Italy in the course of which he studied assiduously. Colet's father was a wealthy London merchant and John was one of twenty-two children, not all of whom survived infancy. John, in fact, inherited his father's wealth, but he nevertheless preferred the life of a scholar to one of luxury and idleness and at Oxford University he delivered a series of lectures on the Epistles of St Paul. In 1504 he became Dean of St Paul's Cathedral in London and founded the famous school which bears that name; indeed, the preparatory department of that school is still called Colet Court to this day. Linacre, Grocyn and Thomas More were already established in London when Colet arrived there in 1504 and this small group of remarkable men were welcome visitors at the court of Henry VII and of his son.

Thomas More was born in 1478, eleven years after Colet and eighteen years after Linacre. His father was a judge and gave the boy a good education. After a brief spell as page to Cardinal Morton, More went to Oxford where he studied the classics, and thence to London where he studied law. In 1504 he was a member of parliament and then resumed his successful legal practice. He was a devout Christian, devoted to the Catholic church, for which, indeed, he was destined to be a martyr.

In the reign of Henry VII, More's chief significance arises from his great friendship with Erasmus, the most outstanding of all the Renaissance scholars of his age. Erasmus was born in the Netherlands, probably in 1466, and became a priest in 1492 after a miserable sojourn in a monastery. He studied in Paris, actually teaching himself Greek, and in 1499 was brought to England by a rich Englishman whom he had been tutoring. Here he met More with whom he immediately became friendly, while at Oxford he encountered Grocyn, Linacre and Colet. Of these four English scholars, he later wrote in glowing terms: 'When I hear my Colet, I seem to be listening to Plato himself. In Grocyn who does not marvel at such a perfect world of learning? What can be more acute, profound and delicate than the judgement of Linacre? What has nature ever created more gentle, sweet and happy than the genius of Thomas More?' Erasmus was no less enthusiastic about England itself during this first visit which lasted only a few months. He wrote to a friend in Paris: 'If you only knew the blessings of Britain! If you are wise you too will fly over here.' He particularly commended the English habit of frequent kissing between male and female friends, though as a priest he should perhaps have been less anxious to enjoy this custom.

Erasmus had one unfortunate experience in England. When he passed through the customs at Dover, his English money, mostly the gifts of his friends, was taken from him because there was a law forbidding the removal of gold or silver from the country; only about £2 was left to him. Nevertheless, he revisited England in 1505, resuming his friendship with Colet and going with him to the famous shrine of Thomas á Becket at Canterbury, a place of pilgrimage ever since Becket's murder in 1170. Then he was employed by Henry's doctor to escort his two sons on a visit to Italy. He did not return to England until he was notified of the death of Henry VII and of the fact that the new king would welcome so distinguished a scholar. On that occasion, Erasmus stayed in England for five years, but his impressions of the country were far less favourable than they had been before.

Though the enduring fame of Erasmus dates from his years after 1509, he had written enough before that date to acquire some considerable reputation. He did not obtain much benefit in the financial sense from his two early visits, but his tributes to his English friends were genuine enough and reflect favourably upon their scholarship. Henry VII would perhaps have been distressed by some of Erasmus' later writings which were highly critical of certain aspects of the Catholic Church of his time, and even more distressed if he had lived to know of the influence which Erasmus had upon Luther, first of the great 16th century Protestant reformers.

Englishmen like Grocyn, Linacre, Colet and More illustrate the influence of the Renaissance upon this country's scholarship and ideas. But there was another aspect of the Renaissance which also affected England. This was the development of geographical exploration, assisted by the invention of the mariner's compass. In 1490 there came to live in Bristol a Venetian called John Cabot and six years later he and his three sons received the king's commission to 'sail north, east, or west and discover and occupy any lands previously unknown'.

Bristol was at this time the most important of English ports and in it lived a number of wealthy and adventurous merchants. They wanted to find a sea passage to the Far East, to Cathay, as China was called, or even to Cipangu, their name for Japan. It is not true that men of this century thought that the world was flat; they knew that it was round, but they did not know that the vast continent of America existed, barring the passage to the east. In 1492 Columbus, in the service of Ferdinand and Isabella of Spain, had made his fantastic voyage and had struck land in what he believed to be the sought-after far east. In May 1497 Cabot and eighteen men set out in one ship to reach Asia as they thought Columbus had done. We should pause here to admire the courage of these early pioneers, nineteen men in a tiny wooden ship exposing themselves to the unknown perils of the Atlantic, at the mercy of wind and weather, uncertain of their destination, poorly equipped and ill fed. On June 24th they found land, possibly Newfoundland but more probably Nova Scotia. From this landfall they sailed south, noting the prodigious shoals of cod off the Newfoundland shore. On August 6th they returned to Bristol, firmly convinced that they too had discovered Asia. Fired with enthusiasm and hope, Cabot set out with a fleet of five ships in the following year. From this voyage he never returned; his exact fate is unknown but it is likely that the entire fleet perished in a gale. Henry VII had taken much interest in this venture; he had met Cabot after his first voyage and had given him £10 with the promise of an annual pension of double that sum. Moreover, Henry contributed a ship to the second, disastrous voyage, nor was he discouraged by its failure. He continued to support the Bristol merchants in their ventures and strongly approved when three Portuguese seamen came to live in Bristol and to assist the English seamen there.

A number of voyages were made in the first years of the new century and there is no doubt that Henry intended that a colony should be established if a suitable site could be found. He rewarded mariners who brought back interesting souvenirs of their expeditions, including birds they had trapped. These 'souvenirs' appear to have included three savage natives who actually appeared in London in 1502, dressed in skins and barbarous in their manners; two years later two of them were still at the court, clad like Englishmen and perfectly civilized.

John Cabot's son Sebastian continued his father's work and made a great voyage in 1508-9, still seeking the elusive passage to Cathay. The king died while Sebastian was still at sea, and he found Henry VIII far less sympathetic than his father had been to voyagers of discovery and colonization.

Henry VII's interest in the sea was not confined to such voyages. He took a lively interest in the Navy and built two very large ships for it, 'The Regent' and 'The Sovereign', each of 700 tons displacement, the Regent carrying no fewer than two hundred and twenty-five guns. These were huge vessels by the standards of the age, and Henry also built three smaller ones. He also had the first dry dock ever to be built in England at Portsmouth, designed and supervised by his capable servant Sir Robert Brigandyne. This was an interest which his son did share and credit for founding the Royal Navy is sometimes given to the second Tudor when it should at least be shared by his father.

It will be obvious that the influence of Henry VII extended very widely in his kingdom. By the time of his death, which occurred on April 21st 1509 at his palace of Richmond, he was only fifty-two years of age. For nearly twenty-four years he had toiled incessantly for his country and for his dynasty and he was so worn out by his labours that contemporaries commented that he looked far older than his years. He was buried in the chapel in Westminster Abbey which he had begun to build in 1503 and which his son completed. In his will he left large sums for religious and charitable purposes, among them the completion of King's College, Cambridge, and of a number of monasteries which he had founded.

Where does Henry stand in the long list of English sovereigns? That he was among the very greatest can hardly be disputed. Professor J. D. Mackie in *The Earlier Tudors* writes: 'He burnt heretics, he consulted astrologers; yet he revived the ancient strength of the English monarchy, and sent it forth upon the path of future greatness He has some claim to be regarded as the greatest of the Tudors.'

He was not, perhaps, a particularly sympathetic or attractive character. Shakespeare wrote a series of plays which covered the whole course of English history from the reign of Richard II to that of Richard III and then collaborated with Fletcher in a play about Henry VIII but he did not dramatize the reign of Henry VII. This reign, with its pretenders and its plots, offers scope enough for a historical play; perhaps it was the personality of the king himself which the dramatist found too drab and colourless for the full exercise of his genius? In his last years there is ample evidence, quite apart from Bacon's critical comment quoted earlier in this book, that Henry became over-concerned with the acquisition of money, and was too willing to use his royal power unjustly for this purpose. Equally unattractive are his projected marriages after the death of his queen, especially that which involved the mad Spanish princess Joanna. Inevitably Henry suffered in his declining years from comparison with his splendid son, described in the following words by the Spanish ambassador in 1507: 'There is no finer youth in the world than the Prince of Wales. He is already taller than his father and his limbs are of a gigantic size. He is as prudent as is to be expected from a son of Henry VII.' To have fathered so magnificent a young prince must have been a considerable consolation to the king, whose life had been marred by the premature death of his eldest boy, Arthur, and of another son, Edmund.

There are those who can find no merit in this man at all and who describe him as an upstart king, cruel and greedy for money. But there are a small minority. More valuable is the opinion of Sir Winston Churchill, himself no mean statesman, in his *History of the English-speaking Peoples*. Volume II:

'His achievement was indeed massive and durable. He built his power amid the ruin and ashes of his predecessors. He thriftily and carefully gathered what seemed in those days a vast reserve of liquid wealth. He trained a body of efficient servants. He magnified the Crown without losing the co-operation of the Commons. He identified prosperity with monarchy... Such was the architect of the Tudor monarchy, which was to lead England out of medieval disorder into greater strength and broader times.'

We may conclude with the historian of 1621, Francis Bacon : 'Yet take him with all his defects, if a man should compare him with the kings his concurrents (i.e. his con-temporaries) in France and Spain, he shall find him more politic than Louis XII of France and more entire and sincere than Ferdinand of Spain. But if you shall change Louis XII for Louis XI, who lived a little before, then the consort is more perfect. For that Louis XI, Ferdinand and Henry may be esteemed the tres magi of kings of those ages. To conclude, if this king did no greater matters, it was long of (i.e. because of) himself : for what he minded, he compassed.'

SUGGESTIONS FOR FURTHER
READING

The Life of Henry VII by Francis Bacon will be found in
any collected edition of Bacon's Works; there is a more
modern biography by Gladys Temperley, published in 1918.
Most writers on this period have drawn upon A. F. Pollard's
The Reign of Henry VII from Contemporary Sources, a
remarkable compilation in three volumes.

There is an essay on Henry VII by C. H. Williams in *The
Great Tudors*; this is not a narrative history of his reign but a
fascinating picture of the man and of the England of his
period. More modern—and equally interesting—is Christopher Morris's chapter in *The Tudors*.

General histories of the Tudor period are numerous and
space permits mentions of only a handful. The Pelican His-
tory of England has a volume on Tudor England by S. T.
Bindoff, the Oxford History of England has *The Earlier
Tudors* by J. D. Mackie, and there is an outstanding work by
G. R. Elton, *England under the Tudors*.

Trevelyan's *English Social History* is as interesting and
informative about the Tudors as it is about all other periods
and is now available in a Penguin illustrated edition.

PRINCIPAL DATES

1457 Henry Tudor born.

1470 Henry fled to Brittany.

1484 Henry forced to leave Brittany for France.

1485 Lancastrian invasion of England; Henry defeated Richard III at Bosworth and was hailed as king (August).

1486 Marriage of Henry to Elizabeth of York (January).
     The Stafford rising.
     Birth of Prince Arthur (September).

1487 Appearance of the impostor Simnel.
     Battle of Stoke (June).

1489 Treaty of Medina del Campo.
     English troops landed in Brittany.

1491 Brittany's independence lost.
     English invasion of France planned.
     Birth of Prince Henry (later Henry VIII).

1492 Invasion of France, followed by Treaty of Etaples.
     Voyage of Christopher Columbus.

1494–5 Poynings in Ireland.

1495 Execution of Sir William Stanley.
     Warbeck well received in Scotland.

1496 Scottish invasion of England.
     Cornish Rebellion.
     Magnus Intercursus.

1497 Battle of Blackheath.
     Truce of Ayton with Scotland.

Warbeck captured in Hampshire.
John Cabot's first voyage.

1498 Death of John Cabot on his second voyage.

1499 Execution of Warbeck and Warwick.
First visit of Erasmus to England.

1500 Death of Prince Edmund.

1501 Marriage of Prince Arthur to Catherine of Aragon.

1502 Death of Prince Arthur.

1503 Marriage of Princess Margaret to James IV of Scotland.
Death of Queen Elizabeth.

1505 Second visit of Erasmus.

1506 Malus Intercursus.

1508–9 Voyage of Sebastian Cabot.

1509 Death of Henry VII (April 21st).

INDEX